Level
2

The Nature Kid's Guide to
SALAMANDERS

DAVID ANDERSON

LP Media Inc. Publishing

For information address LP Media Inc. Publishing,
30012 Variolite St NW, Princeton MN 55371
www.lpmedia.org

Publication Data

Salamanders
The Nature Kid's Guide to Salamanders — First edition.

Summary: "Learn all about Salamanders, the Nature Kid Way"
— Provided by publisher.

ISBN: 979-8-89818-165-9

[1. Salamanders – Non-Fiction] I. Title.

Title: The Nature Kid's Guide to Salamanders

CONTENTS

Soggy Spots 4

World Wide 6

Small Stuff 8

Slimy Skin 10

Sensing Stuff 12

Toxic Tricks 14

Bug Buffet 16

Snap It 18

Watch Out 20

Stay Safe 22

Crawl Along 24

Night Life 26

Solo Stars 28

Dance Time 30

Little Larvae 32

Growing Up 34

Regrow Stars 36

Happy Helpers 38

SOGGY SPOTS

DID YOU KNOW?
Some salamanders never leave their tiny home area. They may live just a few feet from where they hatched!

Plop! A dusky salamander through wet mud. It loves rain!

Salamanders need wet places to live. Their skin must stay moist at all times. They will dry out fast if they stay in the hot sun.

Many salamanders live near freshwater streams. The water there is cool and clean. Rocks and logs give them places to hide. They can also hide under fallen leaves on the forest floor.

Some salamanders live in dark caves. Others hide in damp mountain forests. A few kinds spend their whole lives in cold underground springs. All these damp places help salamanders stay moist and safe.

WORLD
WIDE

Gulp. A Chinese giant salamander rests under a river rock.

There are more than 700 kinds of salamanders in the world. They live on every continent except Antarctica and Australia. But North America has the most: 1/3 of all varieties!

Fire salamanders live in the forests of Europe.

Japanese and Chinese giant salamanders live in cold rivers and streams in Asia. Andean salamanders live high up in the mountains of South America.

The North African fire salamander is the only salamander on the entire continent of Africa.

SMALL STUFF

Snort! A young eastern newt is smaller than a leaf.

Most salamanders are 4 to 8 inches long. Many are shorter than a crayon! The Thorius arboreus is the smallest salamander. It is less than an inch long. It could fit on your fingernail.

But some salamanders grow big. Chinese giant salamanders can grow almost 6 feet long. That is as long as your bed!

Salamanders come in many sizes!

All newts are salamanders, but not all salamanders are newts! Newts are just one special group in the salamander family.

SLIMY SKIN

DID YOU KNOW?
You can see the heart beating through the skin of some small salamanders!

Tip, tap! A fire salamander crawls across damp leaves on the forest floor.

Salamanders have thin, smooth skin. It has no scales or fur. Their skin feels wet and slimy to touch.

The slime is called mucus. It helps salamanders breathe! Salamanders take in oxygen right through their skin. The mucus must stay wet for this to work.

Salamanders also have four short legs and long tails. Their tails help them swim and balance. Some salamanders' tails will even fall off if a predator grabs them. Don't worry though, the tail grows back later!

12

Sniff! A woodland salamander smells the damp forest air.

Salamanders have special ways to sense the world. Most have tiny eyes. They can see movement but not sharp details.

Smell is the most important sense to salamanders. They use both their noses and mouths to smell. This helps them find food and other salamanders.

Salamanders can also feel vibrations in the ground.

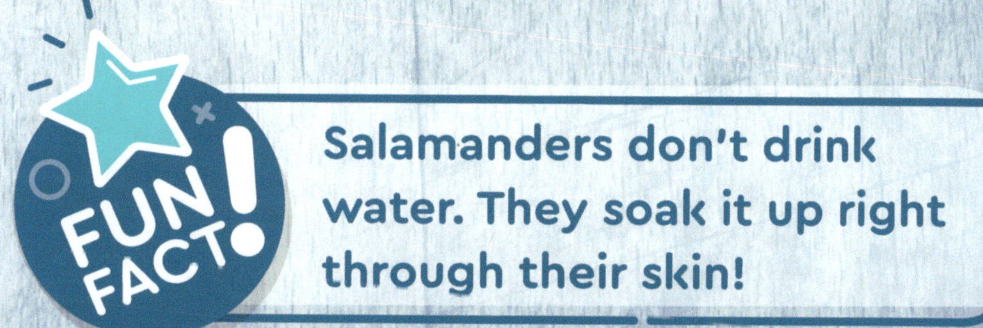

TOXIC
TRICKS

Screech! A spotted salamander shows off its toxic skin.

Many salamanders have bright colors. Orange, yellow, and red all mean danger. These colors warn predators to stay away.

Bright salamanders are often poisonous. Their skin makes toxic chemicals. Biting one will make a predator very sick. It will never try again!

The rough-skinned newt is so toxic that one tiny newt has enough poison to knock out almost any predator.

The slimy salamander (that's its name) makes a sticky white glue. It gums up a predator's mouth!

16

Chomp! A salamander finds a beetle hiding under leaves.

Salamanders eat many small creatures. They love insects like beetles and flies. Worms, slugs, and snails are tasty treats too.

Larger salamanders hunt larger prey. They catch frogs, mice, fish, and tadpoles. The giant salamander can swallow a fish whole.

Salamanders usually hunt at night. They search dark, damp places for food. A salamander may eat several bugs in one night.

Olms are blind, pale salamanders that live in dark caves. They can survive up to 10 years without food and may live to be over 100 years old!

SNAP IT

A salamander's tongue shoots out and back in just 11 milliseconds. That is faster than you can blink!

Whap! A lungless salamander shoots its tongue out at a fly!

Salamanders are ambush hunters. They sit very still and wait. When prey comes close, they strike in the blink of an eye!

Most salamanders catch food with sticky tongues. The tongue shoots out and snaps back so fast, the whole catch takes less than one second! Some salamanders can shoot their tongue out almost as long as their whole body.

Some salamanders hunt differently. Giant salamanders open their huge mouths wide and suck in water and food together like a vacuum. Lungless salamanders launch their tongues like a catapult to snag prey from far away.

WATCH OUT

DID YOU KNOW?
When threatened the Spanish ribbed newt pushes its poisonous ribs through its skin!

Screech! A hawk spots a salamander. It hides under a log.

Salamanders have many predators. Snakes, birds, and raccoons hunt them. Fish eat salamanders that live in water. Frogs and turtles do too.

Shrews and skunks will dig for salamanders. They find them under logs and rocks.

Even large insects are a threat. Giant water bugs can catch aquatic salamanders. Crayfish also grab them with their claws. Life is dangerous for these small creatures!

STAY SAFE

Flop! A rough skinned newt shows its orange belly. Predators back off!

Salamanders stay safe in many ways. Some blend in with rocks and leaves. This is called camouflage. Others dive under water.

Hiding works well too. Salamanders squeeze into tiny cracks. They dig under leaves and mud.

Some salamanders curl up to flash their bright belly, warning predators they taste terrible. Others hold perfectly still and play dead until the danger passes.

Some salamanders scream or squeak! The loud sound scares predators away!

CRAWL ALONG

DID YOU KNOW?
Some salamanders can jump! They curl up tight. Then they spring off the ground. This helps them escape predators.

Crawl! A salamander crawls on the muddy forest floor.

Salamanders may look slow, but they have some cool moves! On land, they wiggle side to side on four short legs. When danger strikes, they can sprint fast!

In water, salamanders are much quicker. Their strong, flat tails push them through streams and ponds. Some even walk right along the bottom instead of swimming.

Some salamanders are amazing climbers! Tree-climbing salamanders grip bark with wide, flat sticky toes. The arboreal salamander can even leap between branches!

NIGHT LIFE

Hoo, Hoo! Little feet move through the dark forest. A salamander is just waking up.

Most salamanders are nocturnal. They sleep during the day and come out at night to hunt and explore.

Daytime is too hot and dry for them. So salamanders rest all day in cool, damp spots like under rocks or inside rotting logs.

Nighttime air is moist and cool. This keeps their skin wet while they search for food in the dark.

Salamanders have big eyes that help them see in the dark! They also use smell to find food at night.

SOLO STARS

Creep! A fire salamander explores the forest floor alone.

Salamanders live alone. Each one stays by itself most of the time.

They do not need leaders or friends. Each salamander finds its own food and hiding spot.

Salamanders meet others only to mate. After that, they go back to living alone. For a salamander, life on your own is the way to go!

Salamanders mark their territory with scent from special glands under their chin. They may fight if another gets too close!

DANCE TIME

Some male salamanders can glow! Under special ultraviolet light, parts of their body light up bright green. Scientists think this helps females spot them in dark, murky water.

Splash! A spotted salamander dances in a pond. He's looking for a mate!

Salamanders mate in spring or fall. Many wait for warm, rainy nights to travel to their breeding ponds. Some travel long distances to reach the same pond where they were born!

Males put on a show to impress females. They wave their tails, dance in circles, and nudge females with their noses. Some even carry females on their backs.

Males also leave scent trails from special glands for females to follow. Once a female picks her mate, she collects his scent package from the ground to fertilize her eggs.

LITTLE LARVAE

Cute! Baby salamanders are growing in their eggs!

Baby salamanders are called larvae. They hatch from eggs in water. Most larvae are very small. Some are only the size of a grain of rice!

Larvae look different from adult salamanders. They have feathery gills on their heads. These gills help them breathe underwater. They also have flat tails for swimming.

Female salamanders can lay many eggs at once. Some lay 50 eggs. Others lay up to 450 eggs! The eggs are soft and squishy like jelly.

GROWING UP

DID YOU KNOW?
Some salamander larvae are so hungry they eat their own brothers and sisters! The biggest babies gobble up the smaller ones.

Plop! Tiny eggs stick to a root floating in the creek.

Most salamander parents do not raise their babies. Mothers lay eggs and leave. This means larvae must take care of themselves from the start.

Larvae find their own food right away. They eat tiny water creatures and learn to hunt on their own.

Some salamanders are different, though. A few species guard their eggs until they hatch. But even these mothers leave after the babies come out. Young salamanders usually become fully grown in 2 to 5 years.

REGROW
STARS

Push! A salamander wiggles away. It has a brand new leg.

Salamanders have a super skill. They can regrow body parts!

A salamander can lose its tail. A new one grows back. Some can regrow legs. Some can regrow even regrow their eyes!

This power is called regeneration. Scientists study salamanders. They want to learn how they do it and see if what they learn can help humans.

Salamanders can regrow the same body part hundreds of times. Imagine getting a new arm every month!

HAPPY HELPERS

Squish! A friendly salamander crawls across wet leaves.

Salamanders need cool, damp places to live. You can help by leaving logs, rocks, and leaf piles in your yard. These make perfect hiding spots for salamanders!

If you find a salamander, look but try not to touch. Your hands can hurt their sensitive skin. If you do pick one up, wet your hands first and put it back where you found it.

You can also help by keeping streams and ponds clean. Never dump soap or chemicals near water. Healthy water means healthy salamanders!

Every kid can make a difference.

GLOSSARY

mucus

A wet, slimy coating that covers a salamander's skin.

vibrations

Tiny shakes or movements that travel through the ground.

camouflage

Colors or patterns that help an animal hide by blending in.

nocturnal

An animal that sleeps during the day and is awake at night.

larvae

Baby salamanders that live in water before they grow up.